Why Sew Blue?

SO-AGU-700

Marco Polo opened the doors of the Far East for his fellow Europeans when he ventured to the Kubla Khan's realm in 1266. The khan, the Mongol emperor of China, soon hired Marco to trade on his behalf with Northern China. The treasures of the Orient were highly prized by Europeans, but the trials and tribulations of transporting the goods was prohibitive for hundreds of years.

The Crusades of the late 11th century through the end of the 13th century widened Europe's trade horizons. The invention of tools for sailing and navigation - the sextant, astrolabe and mariner's compass - made transport of imported goods less treacherous and by 1815 Britain was prominent in the business of trade with the other side of Asia. When China ceded the island of Hong Kong to Britain in 1842, the colony became a bustling port and trade center, the greatest trading and transshipment center of the Far East.

Besides tea, exotic spices and lustrous textiles, the introduction of porcelain to the West was an artful exception to the stoneware pottery so common in Europe at the time. Of particular interest to the upper classes was the pure white porcelain that came only from China at that time. This porcelain was decorated with baked-in cobalt blue patterns, and imitating this form of art became a challenge for the European potters. The earliest imitations of blue and white Chinese porcelain were developed in the city of Delft, in the West Netherlands, in the 17th Century. The pottery was fired with iron oxide to get a purer white.

Once the techniques of firing porcelain were introduced to the potters of England, a few factories were opened to supply the dining rooms of the elite and royalty with decorative table settings. One of the most respected porcelain centers in England was Staffordshire and a descendant of these potters, Josiah Wedgwood, became known as the greatest of all potters.

When Wedgwood entered the field, pottery was still a backward and minor industry, but his specialization - ornamental products - moved the industry from one that provided not only functional items, but decorative ones as well. His skill, tastes and organization skills transformed the pottery industry into one of great importance. Under his expertise, the plain, translucent, unglazed porcelain so common in England developed into jasper ware, best known as a delicate blue pottery with white Greek figures embossed on it. These items - Wedgwood pottery - are still very viable collectibles.

Since their tables were dressed with more elegant plates, cups, saucers, bowls and serving dishes, it is only logical that some precursor of the interior decorating industry took advantage of the situation to begin creating blue and white linens to enhance the table setting. In fact we know that just that happened, and the bluework embroidery technique was transported to the New World.

In Deerfield, Massachusetts, in the 1890s, Ellen Miller and Margaret Whiting discovered some badly moth-eaten examples of blue and white woolen colonial needlework in their local museum. The two women resolved to preserve the technique by reproducing the pieces. They closely studied the stitches and learned to copy them, with the purpose of making only one copy of each item. To insure the pieces had a longer life expectancy, the women used both flax fabric and threads. They even imported indigo dyes to authenticate the color of the stitching in the original antique pieces.

Miller and Whiting began researching the creators of the pieces and could identify seven different designers so various designs were named for them, for example, Polly's parrot and Sarah's leaf. Their endeavors extended to the surrounding area looking for more information on colonial patterns and designs. As their expertise increased, their work came into demand. To satisfy that demand, they formed the Blue and White Society.

The Blue and White Society consisted of several women, some offering to do the work and then waiting to be paid until the piece was sold. Eventually, a variety of linen fabrics and threads were added to the mix. Almost the whole town of Deerfield was involved in reviving colonial arts and crafts with almost forgotten skills. In 1899 the "Deerfield Society of Arts and Crafts" was formed and a yearly exhibit of the various crafts drew large crowds to the town. During World War I, demand for the embroidery waned and the Blue and White Society closed in 1926.

For More Information or Patterns

Laurene Sinema Designs, 3043 N. 24th Street, Phoenix, AZ 85016
Design Originals, 2425 Cullen Street, Fort Worth, TX 76107
Sally Goodspeed, 2318 N. Charles Street, Baltimore, MD 21218
Aunt Effie's Heirlooms, P.O. Box 55374, Madison, WI 53705
Colonial Patterns, Inc., 340 W. 5th Street, Kansas City, MO 64105
Lace Tales, 211 East Hackberry, Fredericksburg, TX 78624
Taylor Made Designs, P.O. Box 31024, Phoenix, AZ 85046
Betty Alderman Designs, P.O. Box 409, Palmyra, NY 14522

MANY THANKS to my friends
for their cheerful help and wonderful ideas!
Art Coordinator-Kathy McMillan
Art Director-Laurie Rice
Production Artist-Jennifer Tennyson
Artist-Charlie Davis/Young
Photography-David & Donna Thomason
Quilters-Eddie Branch, Janie Ray & Virginia Reynolds

Snow Ball Pillow Shams

FINISHED SIZE: 22½" wide x 28½" long

SUPPLIES:
- 44" wide, 100% cotton fabrics:
  - 1½ yards White for blocks and backs
  - 1½ yards Blue for blocks and borders
- 2 skeins of DMC 6-ply embroidery floss to match the Blue fabric
- White sewing thread
- Size 8 embroidery needle
- Sharp No. 2 pencil
- Small embroidery hoop (optional)
- Reynolds Wrap plastic coated freezer paper

CUTTING:
Cut 6 White 7½" squares.
Cut 6 White 6½" squares.
Cut 4 White 16½" x 18" pieces for backing.
Cut 5 White 2½" x 42" strips for squares.
Cut 4 Blue 5½" x 29" strips for the top and bottom borders.
Cut 4 Blue 5½" x 23" strips for the side borders.
Cut 3 Blue 2½" x 42" strips for squares.
Cut 24 Blue 2½" squares for block corners.
Cut 6 freezer paper 7½" squares.

ASSEMBLY:
1. Follow the Basic How-Tos on page 2 to back each 7½" White square with freezer paper and to transfer embroidery designs. Embroider and press squares according to Basic How-Tos. Trim squares to 6½" x 6½", make certain the design is centered on each square.

2. Follow Steps 2 and 3 of the Snow Ball Quilt, at right, to make 12 octagons with the White 6½" squares. Lay the embroidered blocks aside and cut each of the plain blocks in half. Cut 2 of the halves in half again to make 4 small corner blocks.

3. For 9-patch blocks, sew 2 sets of White and Blue strips, sew 1 Blue and White strip set. Cut each set of strips into 2½" pieces. Sew alternating strips of the color combinations together, with right sides facing, to make 12 Nine Patch 6½" squares.

Make 2 ← 2½" wide
Make 1 ← 2½" wide

Sew strips of color combinations together, cut each set into 2½" pieces. Sew alternating strips together to make 12 Nine Patch 6½" squares.

4. Lay 6 of the Nine Patch blocks aside. Cut each of the remaining 6 Nine Patch blocks in half. Cut 2 of the halves in half again to make 4 small squares for corner blocks.

5. Sew 2 rows of half and quarter blocks for each pillow as shown. Sew 2 rows of embroidered blocks, Nine Patch blocks and half blocks as illustrated. Sew the rows together to make each pillow sham top.

6. Fold back ¼" twice along one 18" edge of each of the White backing pieces, press hem in place. Fold back that edge again 1¼". Pin the layers together and sew down the center of the ¼" hem to make a finished edge on each piece. With wrong sides facing, sew the unfinished edges of one of the White backing pieces to the pillow sham front, aligning outer edges. Repeat to sew the remaining backing piece in place. The pieces overlap at the center.

7. With right sides facing, sew the 29" top and bottom Blue borders in place. Sew the 23" side borders in place. Miter corners. Fold back ¼" around all outer edges. Fold the edges to the back. Hand sew the folded edge in place to cover the seams around the edges of the pillow sham. Press the completed pieces.

Butterflies and birds will carry you off to dreamland when you make these pillow shams using Nine Patch blocks and Snow Ball squares. A little cutting, a little sewing and a little embroidery are all it takes to make them!

Patterns on pages 75, 76, 77, 85, 86

Snow Ball Quilt

FINISHED SIZE: 36½" wide x 48½" long

SUPPLIES:
- 44" wide, 100% cotton fabrics:
  3 yards White for blocks and backing
  1½ yards Blue for blocks
- 42" x 53" piece of batting
- 3 skeins of DMC 6-ply embroidery floss to match the Blue fabric
- White sewing thread
- Size 8 embroidery needle
- Sharp No. 2 pencil
- Small embroidery hoop (optional)
- Reynolds Wrap plastic coated freezer paper

CUTTING:
- Cut 12 White 7½" squares.
- Cut 6 White 6½" squares.
- Cut 1 White 42" x 53" piece for backing.
- Cut 8 White 2½" x 42" strips for squares.
- Cut 4 Blue 3¾" x 45½" strips for side borders.
- Cut 2 Blue 3¾" x 29" strips for the top and bottom borders.
- Cut 7 Blue 2½" x 42" strips for squares.
- Cut 36 Blue 2½" squares for block corners.
- Cut Blue 1½" strips for binding.
- Cut 12 freezer paper 7½" squares.

ASSEMBLY:

1. Follow the Basic How-Tos on page 2 to back each 7½" White square with freezer paper and to transfer embroidery designs. Embroider and press squares. Trim squares to 6½" x 6½", make certain the design is centered on each square.

2. Measure 2⅛" from each corner of each 6½" White block. Mark. Cut corners from each block to make 18 octagons.

3. Cut diagonally across each 2½" Blue square to make 72 triangles. Use ¼" seam allowances throughout. With right sides facing, sew a Blue triangle at each corner of each of the White octagons, as shown in illustration. Press toward Blue triangle.

4. Lay the embroidered blocks aside. Cut each of the remaining 6 octagon blocks in half. Cut one of the halves in half again to make 2 corner blocks.

5. For 9-patch blocks, sew 3 sets of White and Blue strips, sew 2 Blue and White strip sets. Cut each set of strips into 2½" pieces. Assemble blocks as for Pillow Shams, at left. Cut 6 of the Nine Patch blocks in half, then cut one of the halves in half again to make 2 corner blocks.

6. Sew embroidered squares alternating with Nine Patch blocks into rows as shown in Assembly Diagram. Press seams toward Blue. Sew top and bottom rows with alternating half blocks, add quarter square corners at each end.

7. With right sides facing, sew the Blue 45½" side border strips in place. Press seams toward the borders.

8. Attach the Blue 29" top and bottom borders in the same manner. Press seams toward the Blue borders.

9. Layer backing, batting and top to form a sandwich. Baste layers.

10. Quilt as desired.

11. Remove the basting stitches. Trim the backing and batting even with the edges of the quilt top.

12. Bind the quilt edges with the Blue 1½" strips, mitering corners.

A pretty combination of octagonal Snow Ball blocks and Nine Patch blocks makes a really interesting quilt!

Patterns on pages 66-68, 72, 77, 80, 82-84, 86, 88, 89

**SNOW BALL QUILT
ASSEMBLY DIAGRAM**

Redwork embroidery teams with Bluework embroidery in this wall quilt to salute the patriotic themes of America's official seal and the stars and stripes. What a great way to honor your favorite veteran!

Patterns on pages 20, 21

Eagle Wall Quilt

FINISHED SIZE: 23" square

SUPPLIES:
- 44" wide, 100% cotton fabrics:
  - 1½ yards White for blocks, borders and backing
  - ¼ yard Blue for borders and binding
  - ¼ yard Red for stars
- 27" x 27" piece of batting
- 1 skein of DMC 6-ply embroidery floss to match the Red fabric
- 1 skein of DMC 6-ply embroidery floss to match the Blue fabric
- White sewing thread
- Size 8 embroidery needle
- Sharp No. 2 pencil
- Small embroidery hoop (optional)
- Reynolds Wrap plastic coated freezer paper

CUTTING:
Cut 1 White 16" center square.
Cut 4 White 5" corner squares.
Cut 4 White 1½" x 15½" strips for borders.
Cut 1 White 27" square for backing.
Cut 8 Blue 2" x 15½" strips for borders.
Cut 4 Blue 1¼" x 25" strips for binding.
Cut 4 Red 4½" squares for stars.
Cut 1 freezer paper 16" square.

ASSEMBLY:
1. Follow the Basic How-Tos on page 2 to back the 16" White square with freezer paper and to transfer embroidery designs. Embroider and press square. Trim square to 15½" x 15½", make certain the design is centered on the square.
2. Trace the star pattern on page 21 onto the right side of each of the Red squares. Cut out stars, adding ³⁄₁₆" seam allowance around all edges. Center a star on each of the White 5" corner squares. Fold back seam allowance on stars and applique in place with applique tack stitches. Press the completed star squares.
3. Use ¼" seam allowances throughout. With right sides facing, sew 2 Blue 2" border strips on either side of a White 1½" border strip. Make 4 sets. Press seams toward the Blue strips.

4. With right sides facing, sew one star square at each end of 2 of the Blue and White strip sets to make top and bottom borders. Press seams toward strips.
5. With right sides facing, sew the remaining Blue and White border strip sets at either side of the embroidered square. Press seams toward the borders. Sew the top and bottom borders in place.
6. Layer the White backing square, batting and assembled top to form a sandwich. Baste the layers together.
7. Quilt as desired.
8. Remove the basting stitches. Trim the backing and batting even with the edges of the assembled top.
9. Bind the quilt edges with the Blue 1¼" strips.

Animals Baby Quilt

FINISHED SIZE: 36" wide x 52" long

SUPPLIES:
- 44" wide, 100% cotton fabrics:
    - 3⅓ yards White for blocks, sashings, borders and backing
    - 1⅔ yards Blue for sashings, borders and binding
    - ¼ yard Red for Nine Patch blocks
- 40" x 56" piece of batting
- 3 skeins of DMC 6-ply embroidery floss to match the Red fabric
- White sewing thread
- Size 8 embroidery needle
- Sharp No. 2 pencil
- Small embroidery hoop (optional)
- Reynolds Wrap plastic coated freezer paper

CUTTING:
Cut 15 White 9" squares.
Cut 6 White 1½" x 56" strips for sashings, side borders and Nine Patch squares.
Cut 1 White 40" x 56" square for backing.
Cut 12 Blue 1½" x 56" strips for sashings, side borders and binding.
Cut 3 Red 1½" x 42" strips for Nine Patch squares.
Cut 15 freezer paper 9" squares.

ASSEMBLY:
1. Follow the Basic How-Tos on page 2 to back each 9" White square with freezer paper and to transfer embroidery designs. Embroider and press squares. Trim square to 8½" x 8½", make certain the design is centered on the square.

2. Use ¼" seam allowances throughout. With right sides facing, sew 2 Blue 1½" sashing strips on either side of a White 1½" sashing strip. Make 5 sets. Press seams toward the Blue strips. Lay 2 sets aside. Cut 3 of the sets into 8½" lengths.

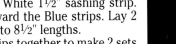

3. Sew Red and White 1½" strips together to make 2 sets of each color combination. Cut each set into 2½" pieces. Sew alternating strips of the color combinations together, with right sides facing, to make 8 Nine Patch 3½" squares.

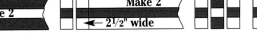

Sew strips of color combinations together, cut each set into 2½" pieces. Sew alternating strips together to make 8 Nine Patch 3½" squares.

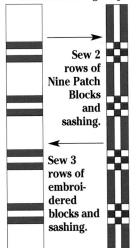

Sew 2 rows of Nine Patch Blocks and sashing.

Sew 3 rows of embroidered blocks and sashing.

4. With right sides facing, sew 4 Nine Patch squares and 5 sashing strips into 2 vertical rows. Press all the seams toward Blue.

5. With right sides facing, alternate 5 embroidered blocks with 4 sashing strips to make 3 vertical rows. Press the seams toward strips.

6. With right sides facing, sew the block rows alternately with the Nine Patch rows as shown in the Assembly Diagram, below.

7. Sew the other 2 border strips at each side of the quilt. Press seams toward borders.

8. Layer the White backing, batting and assembled top to form a sandwich. Baste the layers together.

9. Quilt the quilt as desired.

10. Remove the basting stitches. Trim the backing and batting even with the top.

11. Bind edges with the Blue 1¼" strips.

Cows, kittens, dogs, a goose and an elephant will delight the lucky baby who gets this quilt as a 'Welcome to the world' gift!

Patterns on pages 54-59, 60-65

ANIMALS BABY QUILT ASSEMBLY DIAGRAM

Sunbonnet Sue
Day of the Week Towels

Sunbonnet Sue is a traditional quilt motif. She's doing her daily chores. Use the dish towels or quilt to teach an older sister or brother to read the days of the week - and to help with chores!

FINISHED SIZE: Each towel measures 33" x 36"

SUPPLIES:
- 44" wide, 100% cotton fabrics:
    7 yards of muslin for towels
    6" squares of 7 complementary Blue fabrics for appliques
- 3 skeins of DMC 6-ply embroidery floss to match the darkest Blue fabric
- White sewing thread
- Size 8 embroidery needle
- Sharp No. 2 pencil
- Small embroidery hoop (optional)
- Reynolds Wrap plastic coated freezer paper

CUTTING:
Cut 7 muslin 35" x 38" pieces.
Cut 7 freezer paper 12" x 10" pieces.

ASSEMBLY:
1. Follow the Basic How-Tos on page 2 to back one corner of each piece of muslin with freezer paper and to transfer embroidery designs for each girl 5" above the lower edge of the fabric and 2" in from the left edge. Trace a vee below each girl and trace the patterns for the words below the lines. Embroider the girl, vee and words designs.
2. Trace the outline of the shaded areas of the pattern onto the right side of the Blue squares. Use a different shade of Blue fabric for the bonnet and skirt of each girl. Add a ⅜" seam allowance around all edges. Cut out the applique pieces and sew each in place, using applique tack stitch. Press each embroidered towel.
3. Fold back ½" twice along each edge of each towel. Sew hems in place. Use buttonhole stitches and Blue floss to trim the hemmed edges of each towel. Press towels.

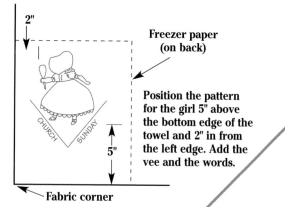

Position the pattern for the girl 5" above the bottom edge of the towel and 2" in from the left edge. Add the vee and the words.

Applique Tack Stitch

Place the needle point just under the edge of the folded fabric and make a tiny stitch.

Patterns on pages 91-97

Sunbonnet Sue One Week Quilt

FINISHED SIZE: 24" wide x 44" long

SUPPLIES:
- 44" wide, 100% cotton fabrics:
  1¾ yards White for blocks, backing and binding
  1¼ yards Blue for sashings and borders
  6" squares of 7 complementary Blue fabrics for appliques
- 28" x 50" piece of batting
- 3 skeins of DMC 6-ply embroidery floss to match the darkest Blue fabric
- White sewing thread
- Size 8 embroidery needle
- Sharp No. 2 pencil
- Small embroidery hoop (optional)
- Reynolds Wrap plastic coated freezer paper

CUTTING:
Cut 8 White 9" squares.
Cut 1 White 28" x 40" piece for backing.
Cut White 1¼" strips for binding.
Cut 4 Blue 2½" x 8½" strips for sashings.
Cut 3 Blue 2½" x 18½" strips for sashings.
Cut 2 Blue 3½" x 24½" strips for the top and bottom borders.
Cut 2 Blue 3½" x 44" strips for the top and bottom borders.
Cut 8 freezer paper 9" squares.

ASSEMBLY:
1. Follow the Basic How-Tos on page 2 to back each 9" White square with freezer paper and to transfer embroidery designs. Embroider squares. Trace the outline of the shaded areas of the pattern onto the right side of the Blue squares. Use a different shade of Blue fabric for the bonnet and skirt of each girl. Add a 3/16" seam allowance around all edges. Cut out the applique pieces and sew each in place using applique tack stitch. Press squares. Trim squares to 8½" x 8½", make certain the design is centered on the square.
2. Use a ¼" seam allowance throughout. With right sides facing, sew an embroidered block on either side of a Blue 8½" sashing strip to make 4 block rows. Press the seams toward the Blue strips.
3. With right sides facing, sew block rows alternately with 24½" Blue sashing strips to assemble quilt top as shown in the photo. Press seams toward sashings.
4. Mark each Blue top, bottom and side border strip 3" from each end. With right sides facing, center and sew the top and bottom border strips in place, aligning marks with the outer edges of the quilt. Press the seams toward the borders.

5. Sew the side borders in place in the same manner as the top and bottom borders. Miter each corner of the borders. Press the seams toward the borders.
6. Layer the White backing, batting and assembled top to form a sandwich. Baste all the layers together.
7. Quilt as desired.
8. Remove the basting stitches. Trim the backing and batting even with the top.
9. Bind edges with the White 1¼" strips.

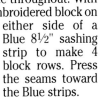

SUNBONNET SUE QUILT ASSEMBLY DIAGRAM

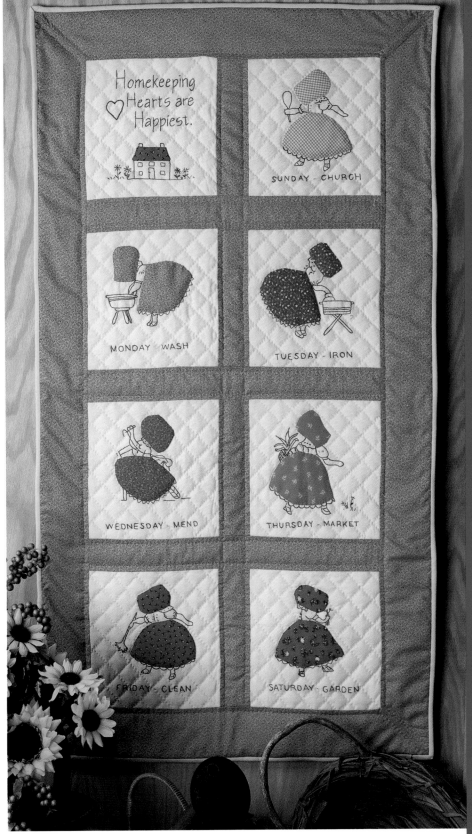

Prairie Point Quilt

FINISHED SIZE: 55" wide x 79" long

SUPPLIES:

- 44" wide, 100% cotton fabrics:
  - 2¼ yards White for blocks, borders and prairie points
  - 2½ yards Blue for blocks, borders and prairie points
- 90" wide, 100% cotton fabrics:
  - 2⅓ yards White for backing
- 60" x 84" piece of batting
- 3 skeins of DMC 6-ply embroidery floss to match Blue fabric
- White sewing thread
- Size 8 embroidery needle
- Sharp No. 2 pencil
- Small embroidery hoop (optional)
- Reynolds Wrap plastic coated freezer paper

CUTTING:

Cut 20 White 9" squares.
Cut 2 White 4½" x 64½" strips for the inner side borders.
Cut 2 White 4½" x 48½" strips for the inner top and bottom borders.
Cut 24 White 4" squares for prairie points.
Cut 1 White 60" x 85" piece for backing.
Cut 20 Blue 8½" squares
Cut 2 Blue 4" x 72½" strips for the side borders.
Cut 2 Blue 4" x 56½" strips for the top and bottom borders.
Cut 24 Blue 4" squares for prairie points.
Cut Blue 1½" strips for binding.
Cut 8 freezer paper 9" squares.

ASSEMBLY:

1. Follow the Basic How-Tos on page 2 to back each 9" White square with freezer paper and to transfer embroidery designs. Embroider squares. Press squares. Trim squares to 8½" x 8½", make certain the design is centered on the square.

2. Use ¼" seam allowances throughout. With right sides facing, sew alternating embroidered squares with Blue squares to make 8 rows. Press seams toward Blue squares.

3. With right sides facing, sew block rows alternately to assemble quilt top as shown in the photo. Press seams open.

4. With right sides facing, sew the White 64½" inner border strips in place. Press the seams toward the quilt center.

5. Sew the White top and bottom borders in place in the same manner. Press the seams toward the quilt center.

6. With right sides facing, sew the Blue 72½" side borders in place. Press the seams toward the Blue borders.

7. Sew the Blue top and bottom borders in place in the same manner. Press the seams toward the Blue borders.

8. Follow the instructions on page 11 to make 24 White and 24 Blue prairie points with the 4" squares. Adjust the prairie points along the outer edge of the Blue side borders, aligning the raw edges. Pin the points in place and sew them in place, using ¼" seam allowance. Fold the prairie points out from the side of the quilt and press.

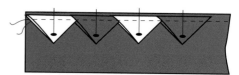

Sew the prairie points along the outer edge of each Blue side border.

Prairie Point Quilt furnished courtesy of Sue Bouchard, Vista, California.

9. Layer the White backing, batting and assembled top to form a sandwich. Baste all the layers together.

10. Quilt the quilt as desired.

11. Remove the basting stitches. Trim the edges of the batting even with the straight edges of the quilt top. Cut the sides of the backing ¼" wider than the quilt top Turn the ¼" side edges of the backing back at each side to cover the raw edges of the prairie points. Sew folded backing edges in place. Trim the backing even with the top and bottom edges of the quilt top.

12. Bind the top and bottom edges of the quilt with the Blue 1½" strips.

Mom said that it's not nice to point, but she'd probably make an exception in this case!
The simple prairie points that trim the sides of this quilt make a point of their own: Something different can be a thing of real beauty!

Patterns on pages 73-77, 80, 85, 86, 88

PRAIRIE POINT QUILT ASSEMBLY DIAGRAM

Prairie Points

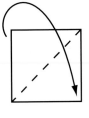

1. Fold the 24 White and 24 Blue 4" squares in half diagonally. Press. folds

2. Fold the squares in half again. Press.

3. Align the prairie points side by side, alternating colors. Tuck one end of the point inside the open edge of the next point.

'Rob Peter to Pay Paul' Whitework Quilt

FINISHED SIZE: 67" wide x 79" long

SUPPLIES:
- 44" wide, 100% cotton fabrics:
  - 6½ yards Blue for embroidery blocks
  - 5 yards White for melon shapes and binding
- 90" wide, 100% cotton fabrics:
  - 2 yards White for backing
- 72" x 84" piece of batting
- 6 skeins of DMC 6-ply White embroidery floss
- Blue sewing thread
- Size 8 embroidery needle
- Sulky White iron-on pen
- White chalk pencil
- Small embroidery hoop (optional)
- Templastic
- Reynolds Wrap plastic coated freezer paper

CUTTING:
Cut 1 template of the large shape on page 98.
Cut 1 template of the melon shape on page 98.
Cut 143 Blue 8" squares.
Cut 310 White melon shapes, using the template.
Cut 1 White 72" x 85" piece for backing.
Cut 17 yards of 1¼" bias strips for binding.
Cut 143 freezer paper 8" squares.

ASSEMBLY:
1. Follow the manufacturer's instructions to use the Sulky white iron-on pen to transfer embroidery designs to 99 of the Blue squares. Embroider squares. Press squares.

2. Place the large template on each Blue square, with the design centered. Use the White chalk pencil to trace the template outline onto the fabric. Cut out the shape.
3. Use ¼" seam allowances throughout. With right sides facing, align the center marks, sew a White melon shape to the top of each embroidered Blue shape. Press the seams toward the Blue shape each time. In the same manner, sew a White melon shape to the left side of each of the Blue shapes.
4. Add a White melon shape to the right side of 12 of the plain Blue shapes. Press seams. Sew a White melon shape to the bottom edge of 10 of the plain Blue shapes. Press seams. Sew a White melon shape to all sides of 1 of the plain Blue shapes. Press seams.

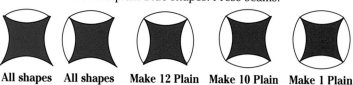

All shapes　　All shapes　　Make 12 Plain　　Make 10 Plain　　Make 1 Plain

Make 12 rows
Use plain (unembroidered) pieces for the top row.
For Rows 2-12, begin with a plain piece, add 9 embroidered pieces, end with a plain side-top-side piece.

Bottom row
Use the 10 plain top-side-side pieces, end with the 4-sided plain piece.

5. To assemble top row, use 10 of the plain 2-melon Blue blocks and add a plain side-top-side piece at the end. To assemble rows, begin with a plain 2-melon Blue block add 9 2-melon embroidered blocks and add a plain side-top-side piece at the end. Press seams toward the Blue shapes. Make 12 rows.

6. Sew on the bottom row, using the remaining Blue shapes. Press.

7. Layer the White backing, batting and assembled top to form a sandwich. Baste all the layers together.

8. Quilt as desired.

9. Remove the basting stitches. Trim the backing and batting even with the quilt top.

10. Bind all the edges with the White 1¼" bias strips.

'Rob Peter to Pay Paul'
is an all time favorite quilt
pattern. Fabric scraps can be
used twice... thus two quilts
can be made from one set of
fabric colors. Cut all pieces
from both colors.
Sew one quilt with large blue
squares and small white
strips (pictured here). Sew
another quilt with white
squares and blue strips.

Patterns on pages 73, 74, 90-97

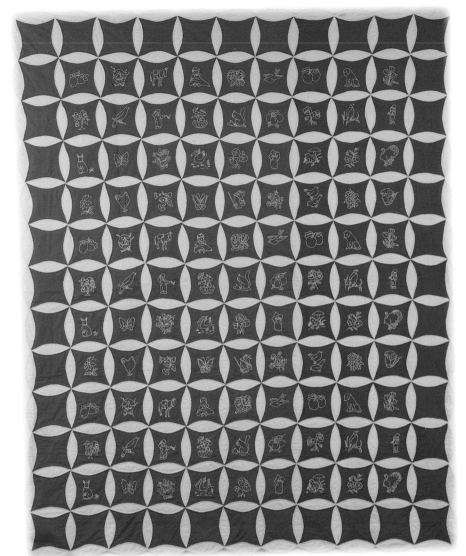

'ROB PETER TO PAY PAUL' WHITEWORK
QUILT ASSEMBLY DIAGRAM

Who says a quilt has to be made of
squares or triangles? This clever pattern
creates circles! Remember to begin and
end with a plain Blue block on each
row. The top and bottom rows are plain
Blue blocks, too. What a pretty frame
for your embroidery!

Helpful Hint

To make sharp, clean corners, come up at A, go down at B. Come up at C (at corner) with needle tip over thread. Go down at D to secure loop at corner, come back up at B.

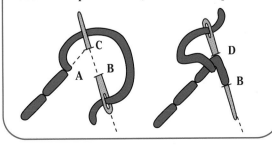

Even though it only has 16 squares, this generous size quilt is a giant among its kind! And the same quilt top is shown on page 2 with a wider border! There will be no more tugging the covers at your house when you create this feather stitched beauty!

Patterns on pages 22-53

Quilt with Large Blocks

FINISHED SIZE (as shown above, at right): 76" wide x 76" long
FINISHED SIZE (as shown on page 99): 96" wide x 96" long

SUPPLIES:
- 44" wide, 100% cotton fabrics:
  4½ yards White for blocks and borders
  2¼ yards Blue for borders and binding
- 90" wide, 100% cotton fabrics:
  2¼ yards White for backing
- 80" x 80" piece of batting
- 4 skeins of DMC 6-ply embroidery floss to match the Blue fabric
- White sewing thread
- Size 8 embroidery needle
- Sharp No. 2 pencil
- Small embroidery hoop (optional)
- Reynolds Wrap plastic coated freezer paper
- OPTIONAL BORDER (pictured on page 2):
  2 yards of Dark Blue floral fabric for the inner borders
  2¼ yards Blue for the middle borders
  2¾ yards of Blue/White floral fabric for the outer borders

CUTTING:
Cut 16 White 18" squares.
Cut 2 White 2½" x 70½" strips for top and bottom borders.
Cut 2 White 2½" x 72½" strips for side borders.
Cut 1 White 80" x 80" piece for backing.
Cut 2 Blue 1½" x 68½" strips for inner top and bottom borders.
Cut 2 Blue 1½" x 70½" strips for inner side borders.
Cut 2 Blue 1½" x 74½" strips for the outer top and bottom borders.
Cut 2 Blue 1½" x 76" strips for the outer side borders.
Cut Blue 1¼" x 76½" strips for binding.
Cut 8 freezer paper 9" squares.
OPTIONAL BORDER - VERSION 2:
Cut 2 Dark Blue 3½" x 68½" strips for inner top and bottom borders.
Cut 2 Dark Blue 3½" x 74½" strips for inner side borders.
Cut 2 Blue 1½" x 74½" strips for the middle top and bottom borders.
Cut 2 Blue 1½" x 76½" strips for the middle side borders.
Cut 2 Blue/White floral 4¼" x 76½" strips for the top and bottom borders.
Cut 2 Blue/White floral 4½" x 96" strips for side borders.
Cut White 1¼" x 76½" strips for binding.

ASSEMBLY:

1. Follow the Basic How-Tos on page 2 to back each 18" White square with freezer paper and to transfer embroidery designs. Embroider squares. Press squares. Trim squares to 17½" x 17½", make certain the design is centered on each of the squares.

2. Use ¼" seam allowances throughout. With right sides facing, sew 4 blocks together to make 4 block rows. Press the seams to one side.

3. With right sides facing, sew rows together to assemble quilt top as shown in the photo. Press seams to one side.

4. With right sides facing, sew the Blue 68½" top and bottom inner border strips in place. Press seams toward borders.

5. Sew the Blue 70½" inner side borders in place in the same manner. Press seams toward borders.

6. In the same manner, add the White top and bottom borders, pressing seams toward the Blue borders, then add the White side borders. Press seams.

7. Repeat to add the Blue top and bottom borders, pressing seams toward the Blue borders, then add the Blue side borders. Press seams toward borders.

8. Feather stitch around the outer edges of the pieced quilt top center, placing stitches 1" inside the inner Blue border. Feather stitch over all the block seams.

9. Layer the White backing, batting and assembled top to form a sandwich. Baste layers together.

10. Quilt as desired.

11. Remove the basting stitches. Trim the backing and batting even with the top.

12. Bind the edges with the Blue 1¼" strips.

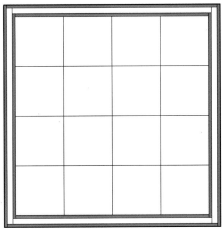

VERSION ONE
Photo on page 14.

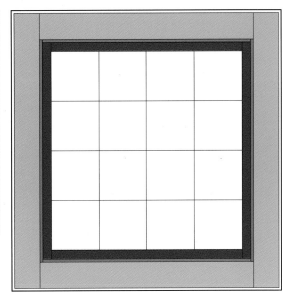

VERSION TWO - Photo on page 99.

OPTIONAL BORDER - VERSION 2:
Inner Borders: Repeat Steps 4 and 5, above, to sew the Dark Blue top and bottom borders in place, then add the Dark Blue side borders to pieced quilt top. Press seams toward borders.
Middle Borders: Repeat Step 6, above, to add Blue middle borders. Press seams toward the Dark Blue inner borders.
Outer Borders: Repeat Step 7, above, to attach the Blue/White Floral borders. Press the seams toward Blue middle borders.
FINISH: Repeat Steps 8-11, above. Bind the edges with the White 1¼" strips.

Lullaby and good night, sweetheart! May the angels watch over you as you dream. And when you wake up, may you be welcomed by the sweet trill of a song bird to start your day! These pillows don't say that exactly, but they mean it!

Patterns on pages 48-51

Sleepy Time Pillow Shams

SUPPLIES:
- Purchased White pillow sham with a ruffle
- 3 skeins of Blue embroidery floss
- Size 8 embroidery needle
- Sharp No. 2 pencil
- Small embroidery hoop (optional)
- Reynolds Wrap plastic coated freezer paper

INSTRUCTIONS:
Follow the Basic How-Tos on page 2 to back the front of each sham with freezer paper and to transfer embroidery designs. Make certain the design is centered on each square. Embroider and press shams according to Basic How-Tos.

OPTIONAL ADDITIONAL SUPPLIES (to make shams):
- 44" wide, 100% cotton fabrics:
  1¼ yards White for blocks
- 2¼ yards of White 3" wide eyelet lace
- White sewing thread

CUTTING:
Cut 2 White 24" x 18" pieces for fronts.
Cut 2 White 16½" x 18" pieces for backs.
Cut the eyelet edging in half.
Cut 2 freezer paper 24" x 18" pieces.

ASSEMBLY:
1. Follow the Basic How-Tos on page 2 to back each White front piece with freezer paper and to transfer embroidery designs. Make certain the design is centered on each piece. Embroider and press fronts according to Basic How-Tos.
2. Use ¼" seam allowances throughout. With right sides facing, sew the eyelet edging around each embroidered front.
3. Fold back ¼" twice along one 18" edge of the White backing piece. Fold back that edge again 1¼". Sew down the center of the ¼" hem to make a finished edge. With right sides facing, sew the unfinished edges of the White backing piece to the sham front, aligning outer edges. Repeat to sew the remaining backing piece in place so that the pieces overlap at the center.

Blue Strippy Quilt

FINISHED SIZE: 75½" wide x 80" long

SUPPLIES:
- 44" wide, 100% cotton fabrics:
  - 3¾ yards White for blocks, outer borders and binding
  - 3¾ yards Medium Blue for sashings and inner borders
  - 4⅔ yards White for backing
- 80" x 85" piece of batting
- 8 skeins of DMC 6-ply embroidery floss to match the Blue fabric
- White sewing thread
- Size 8 embroidery needle
- Sharp No. 2 pencil
- Small embroidery hoop (optional)
- Reynolds Wrap plastic coated freezer paper

CUTTING:
- Cut 40 White 8½" squares.
- Cut 4 White 1¼" x 82" binding strips.
- Cut 2 White 21" x 84" pieces for backing.
- Cut 1 White 42" x 84" piece for backing.
- Cut 2 White 5½" x 68" the top and bottom border strips.
- Cut 2 White 4½" x 80½" for the side border strips.
- Cut 6 Blue 5½" x 60½" strips for sashings and the inner side borders.
- Cut 2 Blue 5½" x 68" strips for the top and bottom inner borders
- Cut 40 freezer paper 8½" squares.

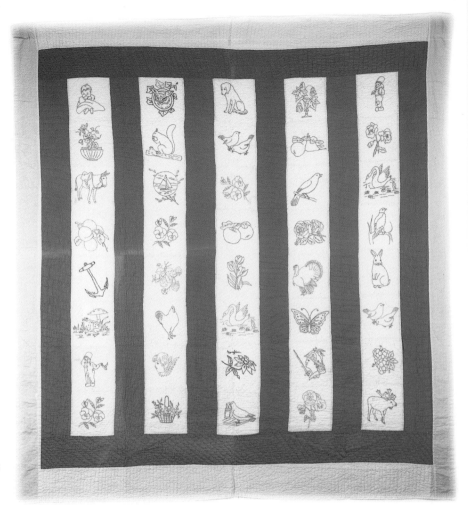

ASSEMBLY:

1. Follow the Basic How-Tos on page 2 to back each White square with freezer paper and to transfer embroidery designs. Embroider and press squares according to Basic How-Tos. Trim squares to 8" x 8", make certain the design is centered on each square.

2. Use ¼" seam allowances throughout. With right sides facing, sew embroidered squares into rows as shown in Assembly Diagram. Press seams to one side.

3. With right sides facing, sew the 60½" Blue sashing strips between block rows and at outer sides of block rows as shown in Assembly Diagram. Press seams toward the sashing strips.

4. With right sides facing, sew the Blue 68" top and bottom border strips in place. Press seams toward borders.

5. Attach the White 68" top borders in the same manner. Press seams toward the Blue borders. Repeat to attach the White 80½" side borders.

6. To assemble backing, sew a White 22" backing piece to each side of the 42" piece, right sides facing. Press seams toward the center piece.

7. Layer backing, batting and top to form a sandwich. Baste the layers together.

8. Quilt all over as desired.

9. Trim the backing and batting to the edge of quilt top.

10. Bind the quilt edges with the 1¼" White strips.

The world goes round and round, but the blocks on this quilt go up and down! It's another twist on the usual method of quilting that says things can be different!

Patterns on pages 67-73, 77-84, 86-89

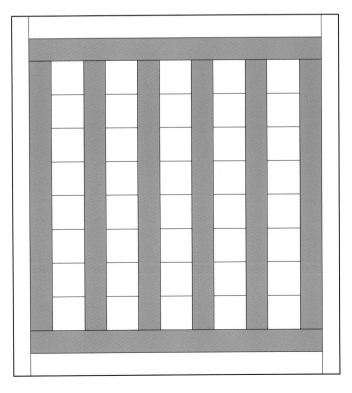

BLUE STRIPPY QUILT ASSEMBLY DIAGRAM

Blue Pillow

Patterns on page 19

FINISHED SIZE: 10½" x 10½"

SUPPLIES:
- ½ yard of muslin
- ½ yard of Blue fabric
- 1 skein of White embroidery floss
- Polyester fiberfil
- White piping

CUTTING:

Cut 1 Blue 6½" x 6½" square for center.

Cut 4 Blue 3" x 3" corner squares.

Cut 2 Blue 4½" x 4½" squares. Cut each square in half diagonally to make 4 triangles.

Cut 4 muslin 3¼" x 3¼" squares. Cut each square in half diagonally to make 8 triangles.

Cut 1 muslin 11" x 11" backing square.

ASSEMBLY:

1. Follow the Basic How-Tos on page 2 to back the White center square with freezer paper and to transfer embroidery design. Embroider and press square according to Basic How-Tos. Trim squares to 5½" x 5½".

2. Use ¼" seam allowances. With right sides facing, sew a White triangle at each side of a Blue triangle. Make 4 sets of triangles. Press seams toward the Blue triangles. Sew one set to either side of the center square. Sew a Blue corner square at each end of each of the remaining 2 sets. Sew these sets across the top and bottom of the center section. Press the pillow front.

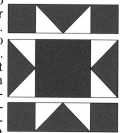

3. Pin or baste the piping around the edges of the right side of the muslin backing square, aligning the raw edges. Overlap the ends of the piping where they meet. Place the assembled pillow front on top of muslin backing square, right sides facing. Sew the pieces, leaving a 4" opening along one side to turn.

4. Turn the pillow right side out and stuff it firmly with fiberfil. Sew the opening closed by hand.

Red Pillow

FINISHED SIZE: 10½" x 10½"

SUPPLIES:
- ½ yards of muslin
- ⅛ yard of Red fabric
- 1 skein of Red embroidery floss
- Polyester fiberfil
- Red piping

CUTTING:

Cut 1 White 9½" x 9½" square for center.

Cut 2 Red 1¾" x 8½" strips for top/bottom sashings.

Cut 2 Red 1¾" x 10½" strips for side sashings.

Cut 1 muslin 11" x 11" square for backing .

ASSEMBLY:

1. Follow the Basic How-Tos on page 2 to back the White square with freezer paper and to transfer embroidery design. Embroider and press squares according to Basic How-Tos. Trim square to 8½" x 8½", centering the design.

2. Sew top and bottom sashing strips in place. Sew side sashing strips in place. Press seams toward sashings.

3. Follow Steps 3 and 4 of Blue Pillow Instructions, at left, to complete pillow.

Birds and butterflies in blue
Fly across a field of white.
Snuggle under this cozy quilt
Keep warm and safe all night.

INSTRUCTIONS ON PAGE 18

INSTRUCTIONS ON PAGE 18

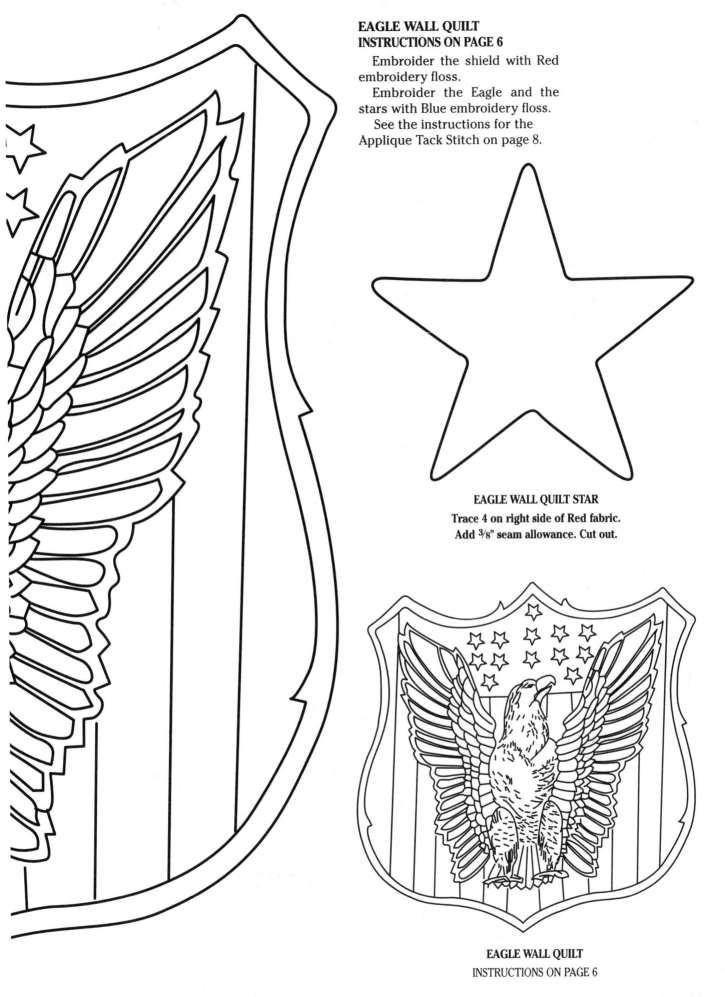

EAGLE WALL QUILT
INSTRUCTIONS ON PAGE 6

Embroider the shield with Red embroidery floss.

Embroider the Eagle and the stars with Blue embroidery floss.

See the instructions for the Applique Tack Stitch on page 8.

EAGLE WALL QUILT STAR
Trace 4 on right side of Red fabric.
Add 3/8" seam allowance. Cut out.

EAGLE WALL QUILT
INSTRUCTIONS ON PAGE 6

INSTRUCTIONS ON PAGES 14-15

Little Mama cat blue
And her sweet kitties, too,
Are quite lovely to view
On a quilt stitched for you.

On a perfect spring day,
We take a walk in the park.
We're prepared for rain.
It's really a lark!

INSTRUCTIONS ON PAGES 14-15

A basket of daisies
Says spring's in the air!
And they'll bloom forever
On a quilt stitched with care.

INSTRUCTIONS ON PAGES 14-15

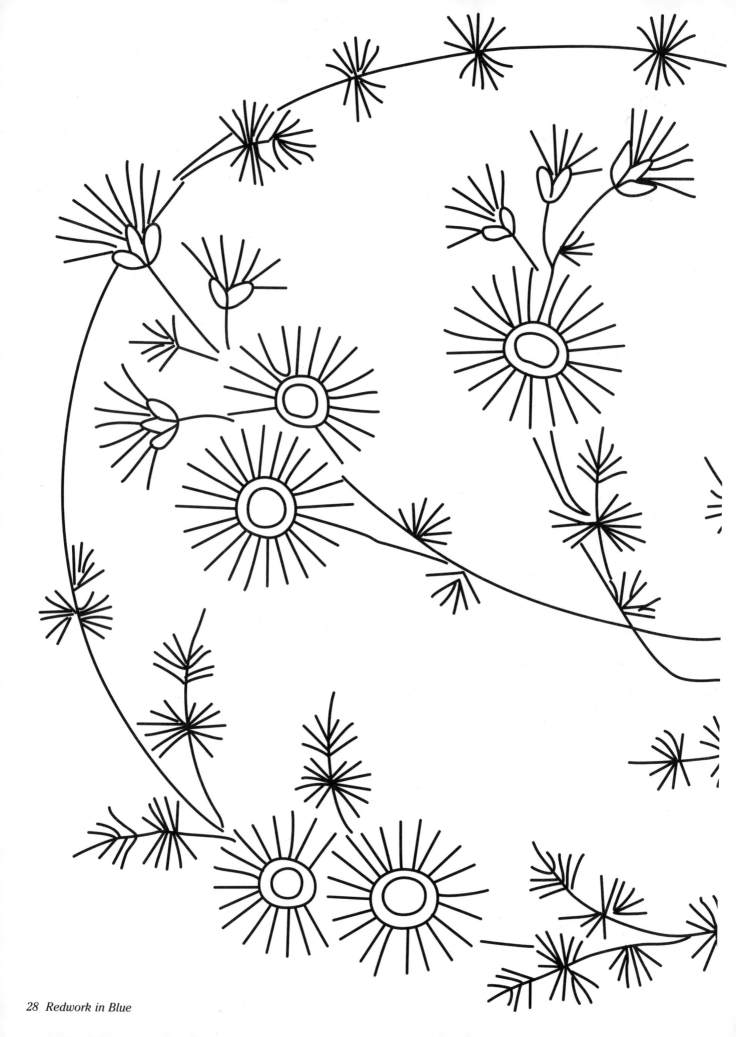

INSTRUCTIONS ON PAGES 14-15

Delicate flowers
Made with stitches straight,
Circle and whirl.
This design's first rate!

A tree,
An owl,
A shiny moon.
It's a perfect scene
From a night in June.

INSTRUCTIONS ON PAGES 14-15

A full blown rose
And buds so tight
Make an elegant quilt
For a long, cold night.

INSTRUCTIONS ON PAGES 14-15

Blue birds of happiness
Fly round the vine,
Gathering flowers
To keep for all time.

INSTRUCTIONS ON PAGES 14-15

Sunflower,
Sunflower,
With bright petals
And seeds,
Blooms in the field.
Many creatures
It feeds.

INSTRUCTIONS ON PAGES 14-15

A bush of roses
Blooms in the light
Luring birds and butterflies
Into joyous flight!

INSTRUCTIONS ON PAGES 14-15

A bouquet of flowers
Is stitched with care.
It brightens the night
With blooms so fair.

INSTRUCTIONS ON PAGES 14-15

A faithful dog is
a child's best friend.
His love and devotion
Will never end.

INSTRUCTIONS ON PAGES 14-15

INSTRUCTIONS ON PAGES 14-15

*Flowers and leaves
In a circle round,
Make a beautiful wreath
Where love may be found.*

A parrot sits upon a stand,
His wings outspread,
His plumage grand!

INSTRUCTIONS ON PAGES 14-15

GOOD
NIGHT

INSTRUCTIONS ON PAGES 14 - 16

OD

GHT

INSTRUCTIONS ON PAGES 14 - 16

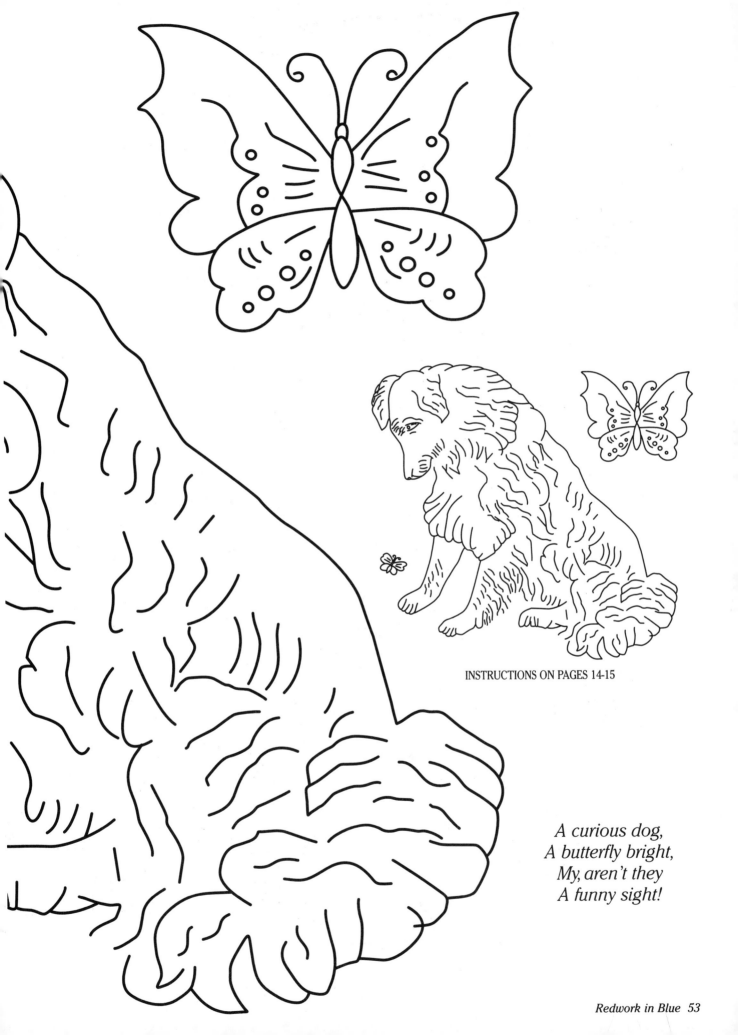

INSTRUCTIONS ON PAGES 14-15

A curious dog,
A butterfly bright,
My, aren't they
A funny sight!

INSTRUCTIONS ON PAGE 7

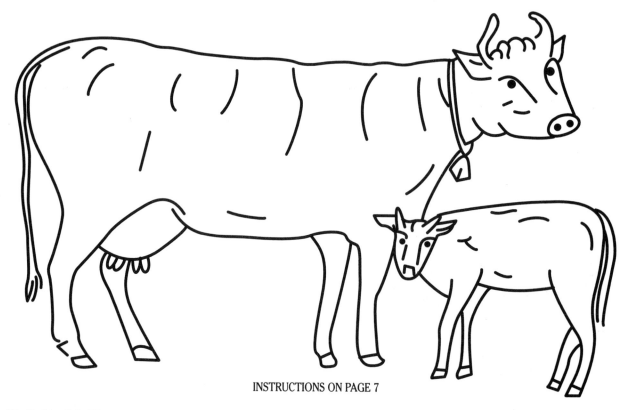

INSTRUCTIONS ON PAGE 7

INSTRUCTIONS ON PAGE 7

INSTRUCTIONS ON PAGES 12-13

INSTRUCTIONS ON PAGES 12-13

INSTRUCTIONS ON PAGE 7

INSTRUCTIONS ON PAGES 12-13

INSTRUCTIONS ON PAGES 12-13

INSTRUCTIONS ON PAGE 7

Dogs are my
Favorite pets,
You see.
They run and
Jump and play
With me.

INSTRUCTIONS ON PAGES 12-13

INSTRUCTIONS ON PAGES 12-13

INSTRUCTIONS ON PAGE 7
INSTRUCTIONS ON PAGE 7

Animals, animals
Everywhere.
Running,
And eating and
Flying in the air!

INSTRUCTIONS ON PAGES 12-13

INSTRUCTIONS ON PAGES 12-13

58 Redwork in Blue

INSTRUCTIONS ON PAGE 7

INSTRUCTIONS ON PAGE 7

INSTRUCTIONS ON PAGE 7

INSTRUCTIONS ON PAGES 12-13

INSTRUCTIONS ON PAGES 12-13

INSTRUCTIONS ON PAGE 7

INSTRUCTIONS ON PAGES 12-13

INSTRUCTIONS ON PAGES 12-13

INSTRUCTIONS ON PAGE 7

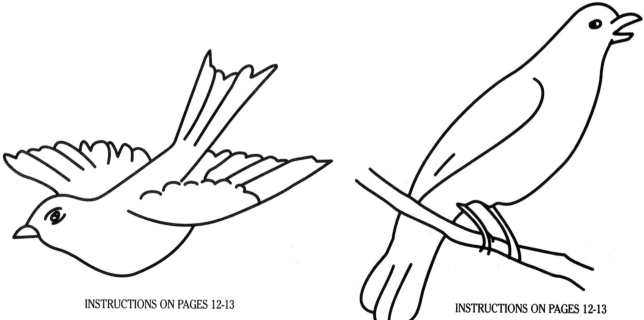

INSTRUCTIONS ON PAGES 12-13

INSTRUCTIONS ON PAGES 12-13

Kitties in a basket,
Kitty on the floor,
Kitties are so cuddly,
Who could ask for more?

INSTRUCTIONS ON PAGE 7

INSTRUCTIONS ON PAGES 12-13

Designs of every shape and size
Stitched with needle and thread
Become a cherished prize
To cover your soft, warm bed.

INSTRUCTIONS ON PAGE 7

INSTRUCTIONS ON PAGES 12-13

INSTRUCTIONS ON PAGES 12-13

INSTRUCTIONS ON PAGE 7

INSTRUCTIONS ON PAGE 7

Strawberries sweet
Sewn with stitches neat,
They're really a treat,
But not to eat!

INSTRUCTIONS ON PAGE 5, 17

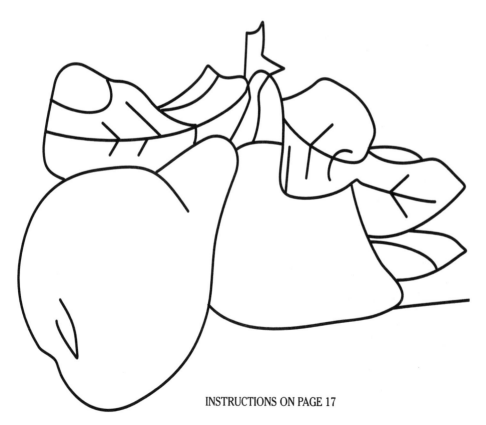

Leaves and pears
Sewn with care
Make a sweet note
On a quilt block square.

INSTRUCTIONS ON PAGE 17

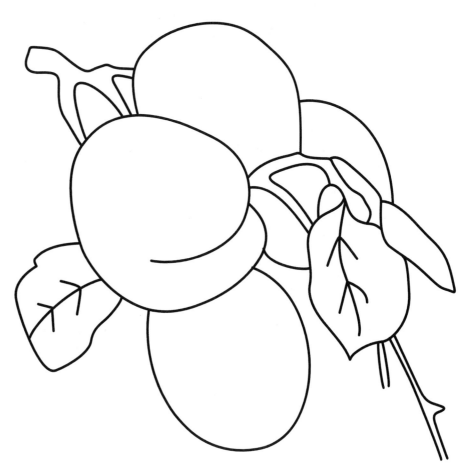

INSTRUCTIONS ON PAGE 17

Grapes and plums
Are purple and sweet.
Stitch them in blue
And they're still a treat!

INSTRUCTIONS ON PAGES 5, 17

INSTRUCTIONS ON PAGES 5, 17

Baskets and vases
Filled with flowers,
Bring memories of gardens
Where you've spent happy hours.

INSTRUCTIONS ON PAGE 17

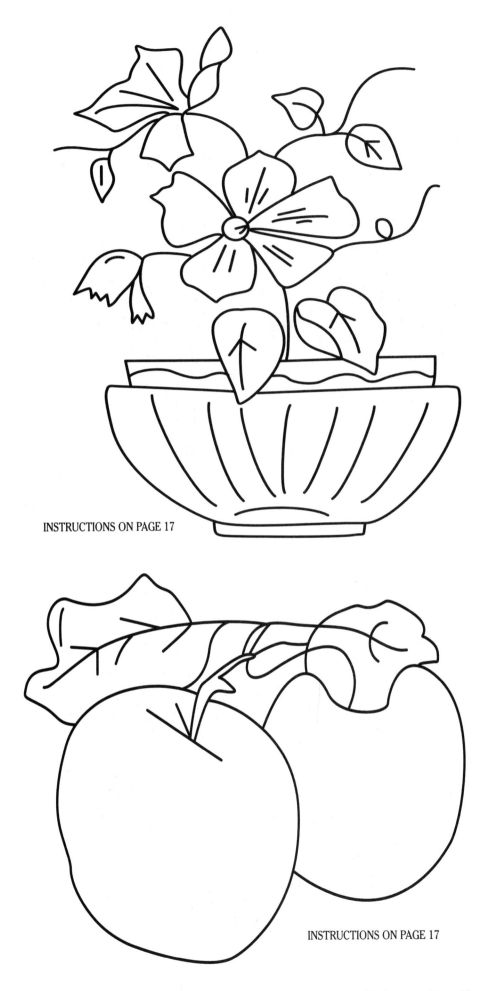

INSTRUCTIONS ON PAGE 17

INSTRUCTIONS ON PAGE 17

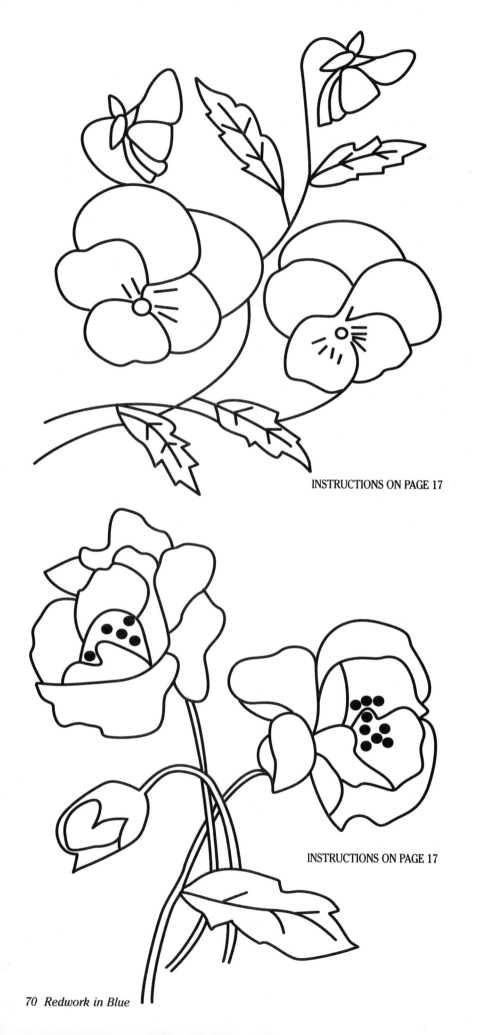

INSTRUCTIONS ON PAGE 17

INSTRUCTIONS ON PAGE 17

INSTRUCTIONS ON PAGE 17

Violets,
Roses,
Tulips,
Poppies!
Blooming in profusion.
Color,
Scent,
Texture,
Beauty,
A spiritual infusion!

INSTRUCTIONS ON PAGE 17

INSTRUCTIONS ON PAGES 5, 17

INSTRUCTIONS ON PAGE 11

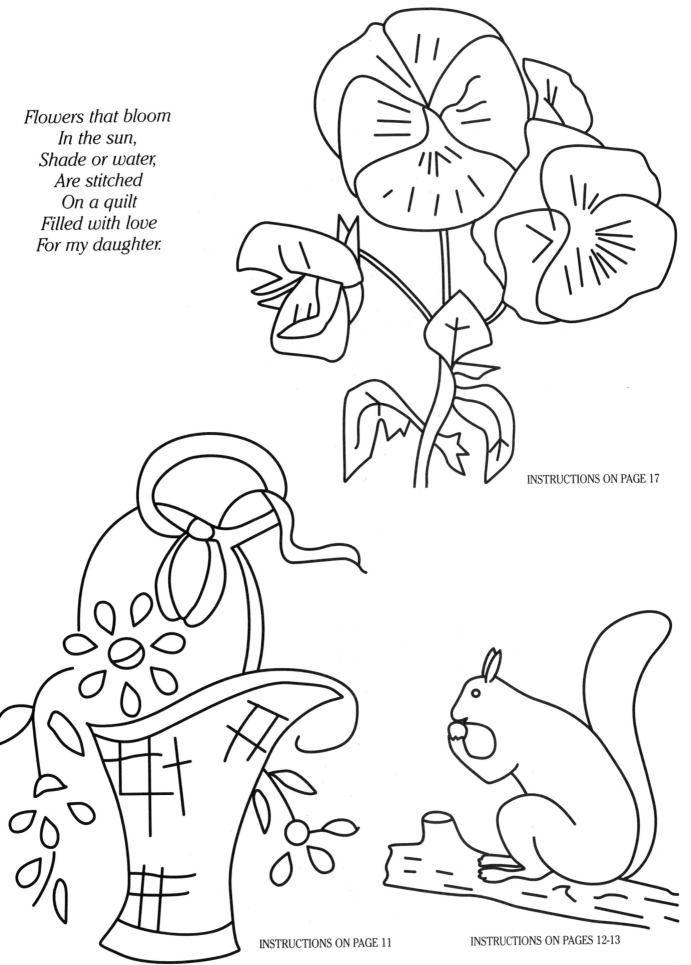

Flowers that bloom
In the sun,
Shade or water,
Are stitched
On a quilt
Filled with love
For my daughter.

INSTRUCTIONS ON PAGE 17

INSTRUCTIONS ON PAGE 11

INSTRUCTIONS ON PAGES 12-13

INSTRUCTIONS ON PAGE 11

INSTRUCTIONS ON PAGES 12-13

INSTRUCTIONS ON PAGES 12-13

INSTRUCTIONS ON PAGE 11

INSTRUCTIONS ON PAGES 4, 11

INSTRUCTIONS ON PAGE 11

INSTRUCTIONS ON PAGES 4, 11

INSTRUCTIONS ON PAGES 4, 5, 17

INSTRUCTIONS ON PAGES 12-13

Butterflies, butterflies
Flit through the air,
Stitch them in blue
For a quilt so fair.

INSTRUCTIONS ON PAGES 12-13

INSTRUCTIONS ON PAGES 4, 11

INSTRUCTIONS ON PAGE 17

INSTRUCTIONS ON PAGE 17

INSTRUCTIONS ON PAGE 17

*Children, children
From far and near,
Each one is a treasure
And ever so dear!*

INSTRUCTIONS ON PAGE 17

INSTRUCTIONS ON PAGE 17

INSTRUCTIONS ON PAGE 11

INSTRUCTIONS ON PAGE 17

INSTRUCTIONS ON PAGES 5, 17

*In the woods we find
Animals of every kind.
Stitch the ones
You remember well.
Make a quilt
To tell the tale.*

INSTRUCTIONS ON PAGE 17

INSTRUCTIONS ON PAGES 5, 17

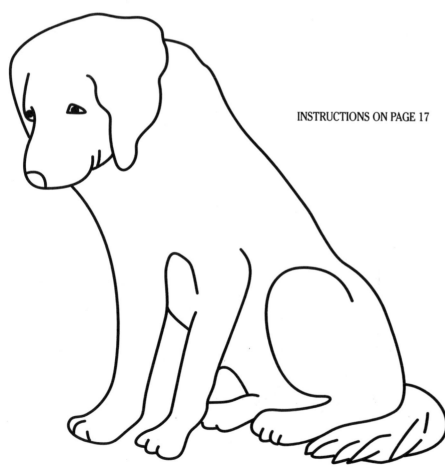

INSTRUCTIONS ON PAGE 17

INSTRUCTIONS ON PAGES 5, 17

Memories of sailing
On the ocean blue,
Preserve them in stitches
For me and for you!

INSTRUCTIONS ON PAGE 17

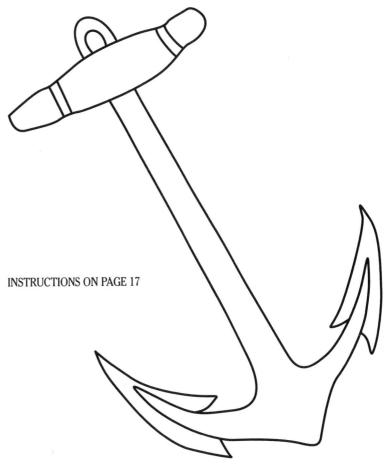

INSTRUCTIONS ON PAGE 17

Birds of prey
Are an awesome sight.
Whether at rest
Or in graceful flight.

INSTRUCTIONS ON PAGE 17

Song bird music
Fills my heart with joy.
It's a sound I've cherished
Since I was a boy.

INSTRUCTIONS ON PAGE 11

INSTRUCTIONS ON PAGES 4, 11

INSTRUCTIONS ON PAGES 5, 17

INSTRUCTIONS ON PAGES 4, 11

INSTRUCTIONS ON PAGE 11

Birds hold a beautiful
Place on the earth,
Helping us, feeding us,
Scattering seeds for new birth.

INSTRUCTIONS ON PAGE 17

INSTRUCTIONS ON PAGES 5, 17

INSTRUCTIONS ON PAGE 11

INSTRUCTIONS ON PAGE 17

INSTRUCTIONS ON PAGES 5, 17

Swans,
Chickens,
Song birds
Unique.
Sounds,
Colors.
The world of birds
Is a sensory treat.

INSTRUCTIONS ON PAGES 5, 17

Homekeeping ♥ Hearts are Happiest.

INSTRUCTIONS ON PAGE 9

INSTRUCTIONS ON PAGES 12-13

INSTRUCTIONS ON PAGES 12-13

INSTRUCTIONS ON PAGE 9

Sunbonnet Sue
Dressed in blue
Works through the week.
Ask her what to do.

MONDAY - WASH

INSTRUCTIONS ON PAGES 12-13

INSTRUCTIONS ON PAGES 12-13

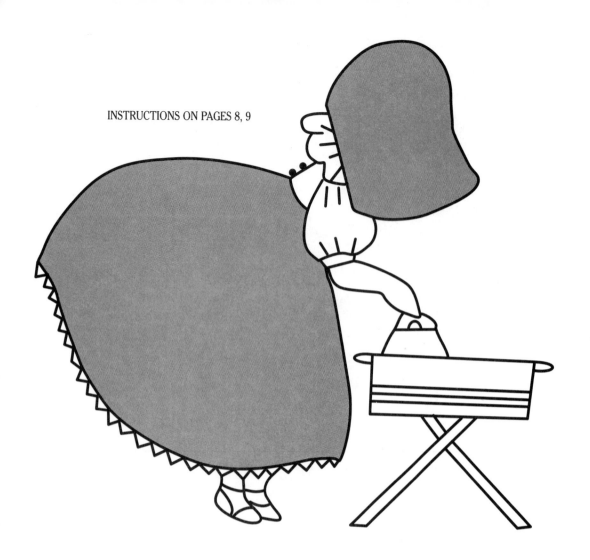

INSTRUCTIONS ON PAGES 8, 9

TUESDAY - IRON

INSTRUCTIONS ON PAGES 12-13

INSTRUCTIONS ON PAGES 12-13

INSTRUCTIONS ON PAGE 9

WEDNESDAY - MEND

INSTRUCTIONS ON PAGES 12-13

INSTRUCTIONS ON PAGES 12-13

INSTRUCTIONS ON PAGE 9

THURSDAY - MARKET

INSTRUCTIONS ON PAGES 12-13

INSTRUCTIONS ON PAGES 12-13

INSTRUCTIONS ON PAGE 9

FRIDAY - CLEAN

INSTRUCTIONS ON PAGES 12-13

INSTRUCTIONS ON
PAGES 12-13

INSTRUCTIONS ON PAGE 9

SATURDAY - GARDEN

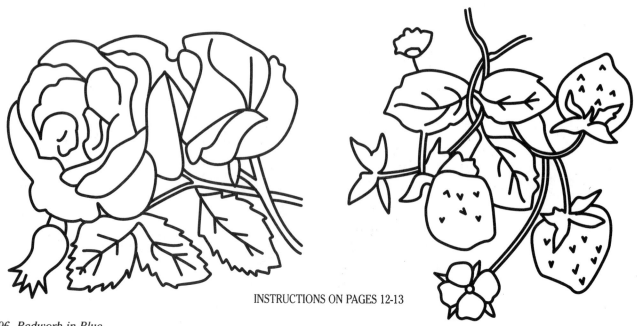

INSTRUCTIONS ON PAGES 12-13

INSTRUCTIONS ON PAGES 8, 9

SUNDAY - CHURCH

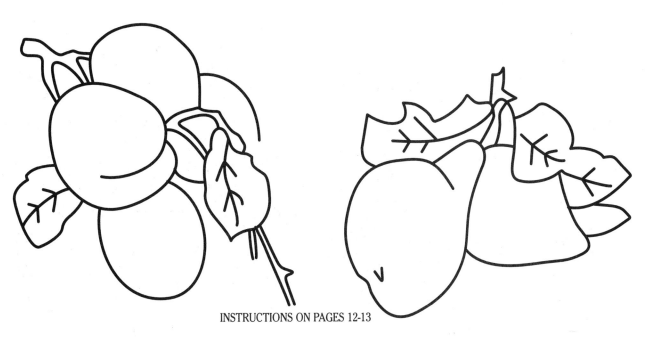

INSTRUCTIONS ON PAGES 12-13

'ROB PETER TO PAY PAUL' QUILT TEMPLATES

INSTRUCTIONS ON PAGES 12-13

Center
LARGE TEMPLATE
Cut 44 plain Blue
Cut 99 embroidered Blue
Center
Center
Center

Center
MELON TEMPLATE
Cut 310 White
Center

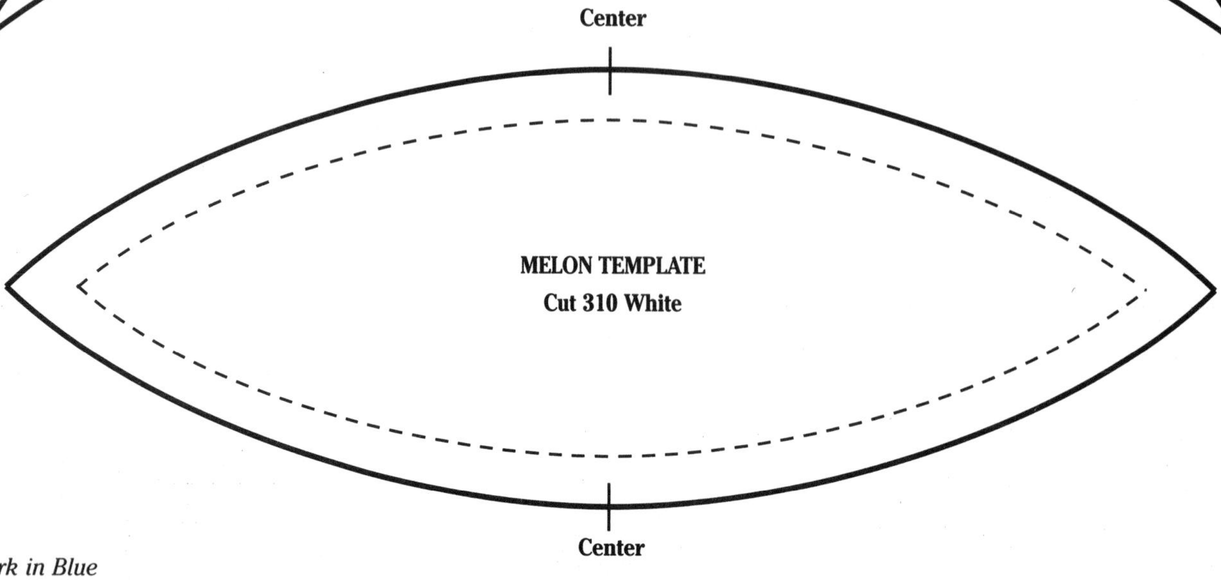

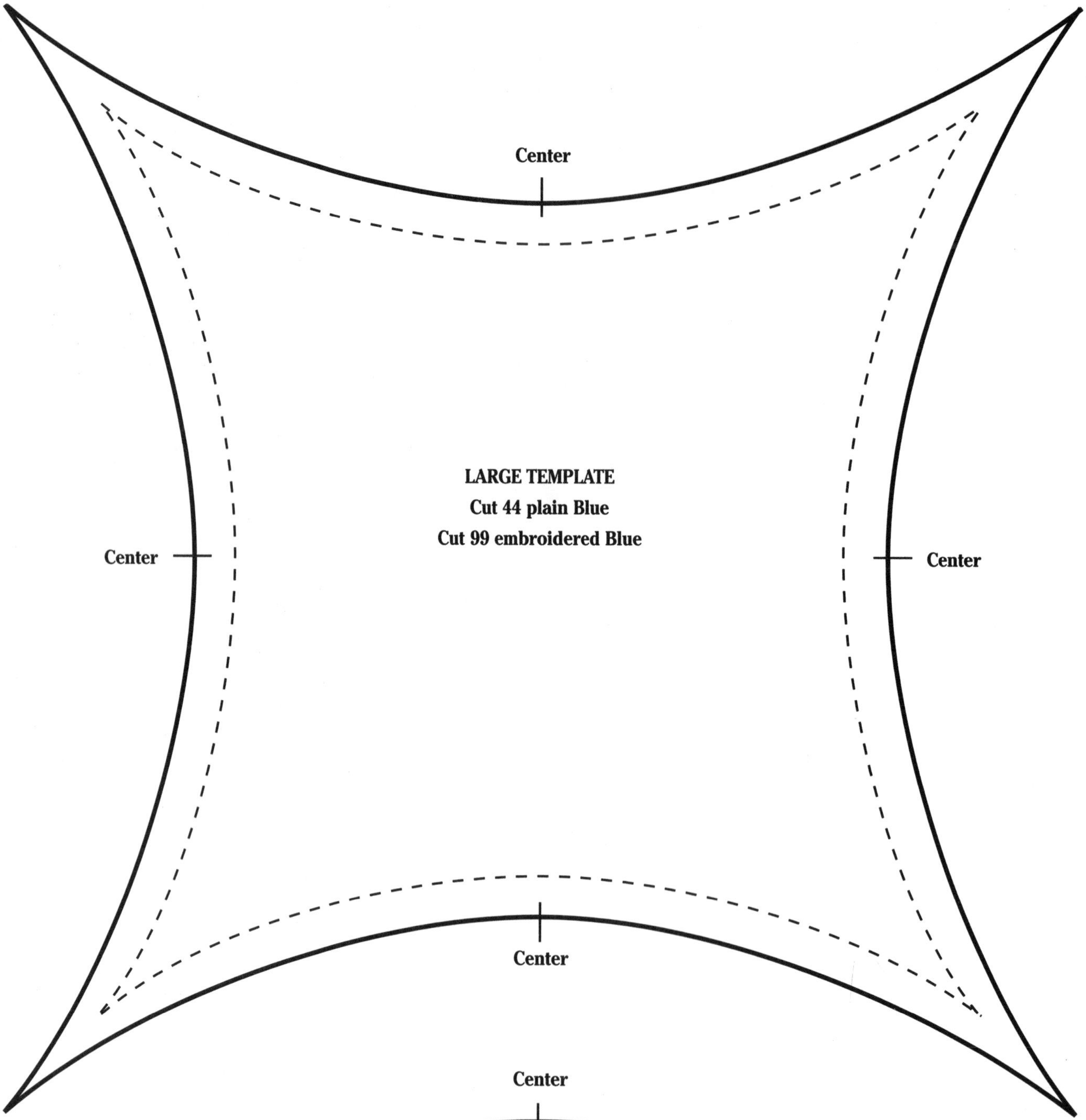